Table of Contents

Full off Your Love

My life is filled with joy and laughter

My soul is no longer cold

You left a mole that makes me feel that we can grow
old together

I wish I could fold you up and put you in my pocket

I bet you don't know how much I want to grow old
and share my life with you

Together we shall remain forever

Never will I lose you

On Earth we grow and laugh

In heaven we must have smiles as we watch the ones
we love

Forever is near

You my dear are close to my heart

Even though I know someday we too shall part

But never will I forget you

Your love is true

My Pain

With all my pain

There comes a strain

It feels tight and has a hold on me

I know it is not right, but it is so hard to fight

The pain is so deep

I am drowning

It makes me want to run and hide

Like hide and go seek

I don't confide in no one

People are not to be trusted

Busted, Busted

All your secrets out in the open

Social Media, Channel 4 news, and now you have
the blues

You lose again

Big regrets; you wish you would have listened when
mama said trust no one

The big lesson, you have been missing

Now you are screaming

Lord how I need a blessing

People keep messing with me

Down to your knees you drop

Begging and pleading

Trust me, he hears you, but he will never mislead
you nor tell your secrets

The only friend you have is in Jesus

My Heart

I give you my heart

I give you my world

Nothing on Earth can pull us apart

I love you long

I love you hard

Nothing in life can go wrong

Loving you strong

Gives me life that last long

As time pass on

I always feel that we shall someday be one

For you are the sun in my sky that shines so bright

You light up my life

I am glad to be your wife

The Pain I Feel

The pain I feel just won't heal

I am scared on the inside

I just want to hide

My life is like hell

You can smell the burned body that lies on side of
you

Can you see the ashes?

Do you hear the cries? Over and Over

I try to tell myself that someday things will get better?

But when will I heal?

When will I smile?

When Will I become better?

Someday I someday

Is This Life?

This is not life this is not love

Sometimes I wonder why the man up above would
allow my heart to hurt

Make me feel low as dirt

As I carry this pain

My eyes water like rain

I feel the strain of pain that leaves me empty within

Is this life or is this right?

Why must I hurt and feel like dirt?

The Shame, Anger, & Pain

I carry scars from those I love the most

I carry baggage from the loss of life

I carry hurt and fear that I can't ever be a wife

My life has been carried by pain, hurt, and anger

My life is hard, rough, and very tough

Carrying scars, wounds, and bad memories that
wouldn't fade, but last forever

I am afraid of my future because of my past

How long will it last?

Will I be strong enough to fight or will I give up
tonight?

Crazy in Love

One moment I hate you

The next I love you, I can't stand you, but you know
you my boo

Thanks to you I have Lee Lee

She's my baby

This roll-a-coaster I am on is driving me insane

It's hard to explain

All I know is that I love you

Can't and won't be without you

Sometimes we have more downs than ups, but you
still around

It sounds crazy but it's true

Yea this love we have can't ever be through

I will love you until I am blue in the face dead in my
own space

If I am not yelling in your face I am screaming your
name like you are Maze

I am your biggest fan

One day you will take my hand

And forever be my man

Yes, yes this is my fairy tale and it ends with you being my man

Boo I will always love you

My Baggage

I carry this baggage

Yes a full package from UPS

It's a mess, watch it, it's fragile like glass, it will crack
real fast

I wear a mask just like Halloween

But between the mask and my face is a blank space

That nothing can fill

I am empty and hurt

Full off emotions

My shirt is wet from tears

I can't erase the pain, hurt, nor sorrow, but I can ask
God to make me strong

It's wrong to hurt the one you love, but hell what is
love

All I feel is pain

Make this rain from my eyes dry or run away like the
shame you bought to me

Others get high (smoking weed)

I just get by

Sometimes I wish I could fly far away from here

And just disappear

How Carelessly

I gave you my heart

Carelessly you didn't notice

You ignored all the signs of love

You wore me out like a glove

I thought together forever

Now it's never

I won't turn back

I can't go back through pain

I sat up at night

My eyes watered like rain

Someday the sun will shine again

It won't be because of us together

It would be because I made it through the weather

Like a bird I am free

Like a bee you stung me

Now it's bye forever!!!

Hard Work

I work so hard for what I have

Nothing is giving to my in a card or on a platter

No father no mother

Everything hard

I live life with a sword

I can't lose

I must choose my path wisely

If I walk away from you

It's because I don't want to go astray

All I can do is pray for you

Friends have become my enemy

They send me their worse

They put a curse on my life

I take it like a grain of rice

Some are in my life for a season

Some for a reason

I don't question the man above

I know he shows love

I wasn't put here for you to love

But to marry my mate and fly like doves

God knows my faith

He truly has my back

With no knives, no weapons ha ha

No weapons formed against me shall prosper it won't work (Fred Hammond)

What's Real from What's Fake

Caught in the crossfire

What's real from what's fake

Do I take what I want?

Stay humble and not mumble

God knows all

He sees his child's flaws and falls

I am a human much more a sinner

Just trying to be a winner

People around me not down for me

Sometimes I allow my emotions to win

Done been here before all over again

One two

Dam here we go again

Slow fast

Cast a spell

Lakisha is out, I tried to warn them

Somebody shout

I am running wild and screaming and hurting

The pain won't heal

I am bruised and full of guilt

The past is here

I fear nothing but God

I fight for what I want

Hunt all men like they are prey

I tried to tell them to stay in their lane

Once again no one is a friend

Caught in the crossfire what's real from what's fake

A Mother's Love

The love of a mother can never be replaced

It can never be erased

In life's race we only get one mother

To hold, love, trust, and to honor

There will never be another

God creates one of us all

One smiles, one style, and that is truly wild

As I watch others embrace love I see smiles on their face

Some never knew what a mother's love is or was
(Grandpa)

Cause the mother they had was taken away in an instance

Now there is a distance (six feet)

No one to hug, kiss, just someone to miss

The longing for her smile, her embrace, or a chance to see her face

Someday in heaven we shall meet again

As long as your mother is here hold her dear and near to your heart

Again and Again

Here we go again

All I see is you

Can't be with no one but you

Can't even see past you

For some strange reason you shall always be my boo

The love we had was true

The day we split

I missed you for days that turned into weeks

Weeks turned into months

Months turned into years

I always thought of you

I missed the scent of your cologne

I wondered what I did wrong

How could this be true?

What could I do to get back to you?

Again and Again I rehearsed these lines in my head

I went to bed and dreamed of you every night

Sometimes I thought you might be next to me when
I wake up

All a dream all a dream

I even thought of hitting you up, but my pride would
not let me

I had a big ego and an even a friend with an even
bigger ego

She put things in my head and say never let him see
your weaker side

Again and Again I allowed time fly bye

All I could do is long for you to cross my eye so I
could tell you sweet things

And sang Rick Ross "You the Boss"

Again and Again I think to myself I loss I loss

I toss you out and any girl could have you

You may be gone and loss forever!!

Take a Stand

Take a stand

Be a man

Don't delay

Time waits on no one

Someone's life is done

A mother's cries have just begun

A father's emotions are on the run

Now he has a gun

He is not thinking

All he knows is that he wants someone to feel what
he feels

The gun he has

He is ready to use it

He is vicious

He is angry

This is the cycle of violence in the N.O.

No one wants to let go

Pride, egos, and emotions

When will it end?

No one knows

All I know is how it begins, never how it ends

No one knows, but someone must take a stand

We must band together like glue

Or forever lose and be blue

Violence is the true disaster that hit New Orleans not Katrina

Think about all the dreams

our kids have.....

Are they worth saving

or just delaying?

You be the judge

There is no denying what the problems are

We all know far more than what we are saying

Our city is worth saving

So put the guns down and take a stand!!

Calling of Angels

(Written for a close family member when God called home an angel)

God takes his angels when we are not ready.

He knows the perfect time, place, and date.

He chooses them wisely.

Your mother was hand-picked the day she was born to be an angel.

As she watched you grow, laugh, and cry she knew someday she would leave you.

This would be one of the toughest jobs ever, but it would be the best thing she has ever done.

God was teaching her then to be your family's guardian angel.

Being an angel is a big job and not many are chosen.

He chooses those who are gentle, kind, soft, and patient with big hearts.

She was that special ONE!!!!!!!

See on the day she left it was because she was ready to graduate and get her angel wings.

On that day she pressed the GPS (GOD Please Save) me button, God knew her work on Earth was done.

She did all she could on Earth.

Now the time had come for her to Guard your life and God aligned time perfectly so that she could be your angel.

So, when you were late for work yesterday, she save you from an accident.

When you didn't make it to the store it was because she was saving you from an armed robbery. She had to leave here to save you.

So smile because God chose the perfect person to be your Guardian Angel.

www.ingramcontent.com/pod-product-compliance
Lightning Source LLC
Chambersburg PA
CBHW081641040426
42449CB00014B/3404